THE WALTZ
OF THE
TOREADORS

by Jean Anouilh

Translated by LUCIENNE HILL

COWARD-McCANN, Inc.

NEW YORK

The *Waltz of the Toreadors* opened in New York January 17, 1956, at the Coronet Theatre with the following cast:

CHARACTERS

(In order of appearance)

MME. ST. PÉ	*Mildred Natwick*
GENERAL ST. PÉ	*Ralph Richardson*
GASTON, *his secretary*	*John Stewart*
SIDONIA, *his daughter*	*Mary Grace Canfield*
ESTELLE, *another daughter*	*Sudie Bond*
DOCTOR BONFANT	*John Abbott*
FIRST MAID	*Frieda Altman*
MLLE. DE ST.-EUVERTE	*Meriel Forbes*
MME. DUPONT-FREDAINE	*Louise Kirtland*
FATHER AMBROSE	*William Hansen*
NEW MAID	*Helen Seamon*

The *Waltz of the Toreadors* was produced by Robert Whitehead and The Producers Theatre

Directed by Harold Clurman

Designed by Ben Edwards

The action of the play takes place in the home of General Saint Pé in France, about 1910.

ACT ONE

ACT ONE

SCENE ONE

The GENERAL'S *room adjoining his wife's bedroom. Exotic trophies, weapons, hangings. The communicating door is open. The* GENERAL *is at his desk, writing. A shrill voice issues from next door.*

GENERAL'S WIFE:
Off.
Leon!

GENERAL:
Yes!

VOICE:
What are you doing?

GENERAL:
Working.

VOICE:
Liar You are thinking. I can hear you. What are you thinking about?

9]

GENERAL:

You.

VOICE:

Liar. You are thinking about women being beautiful, and not feeling all alone in the world for a while, you told me so once.

GENERAL:

I haven't the faintest recollection of it. Go to sleep, my love. You will be tired later.

VOICE:

I am only tired, only ill, because of you! Ill with thinking, always thinking of all the things I know you're doing!

GENERAL:

Come now, my love, you exaggerate, as usual. The whole time you have been ill, and that makes years now, I haven't left this room, sitting here glued to this chair dictating my memoirs, or pacing about like a bear in a cage, and well you know it.

VOICE:

I feel ill with thinking of all the things you are busy doing in your head while you pretend to comfort me. Admit it, hypocrite! Where were you just now in your head? With what woman? In which kitchen, tumbling Heaven knows what drab that scrubs away there on all fours? And you creep up on her, like a great tomcat. Leon, you make me sick!

[10

GENERAL:

By Hades, Madam, you are dreaming! I am sitting at my desk, writing to M. Poincaré.

VOICE:

He's a good excuse, Poincaré! You are holding your pen, oh, yes—but in your head, your hands are still mauling that girl. Stop it, Leon!—if you don't want my death on your conscience. Have you no shame, man, no refinement?

GENERAL:

Will you let me finish my letter in peace.

VOICE:

Whimpering.

But inside! Inside your head! Why won't you let me inside your head, just once—just for a minute?

GENERAL:

Confound it, Madam, my head is out of bounds! It's the one spot where I can have a bit of peace, I want it to myself.

VOICE:

I shall get into it one day. I shall come upon you there when you least expect it and I shall kill you!

GENERAL:

All right. In the meantime—you have brought it on yourself—I shall take Dr. Bonfant's advice and shut the door.

VOICE:

Leon, I forbid you! Leon, I shall have an attack!
In spite of her shrieks the GENERAL *closes the
door. The* SECRETARY *enters in the course of
this punitive expedition.*

GENERAL:

Implacable! I have shut her door! Good morning, my
boy.

SECRETARY:

Good morning, sir.

GENERAL:

My word, she needn't think I'm going to put up with
her whims forever. Haven't you a wife, young man? A
little girl friend—it's the old, old story—you meet her
by chance, you take her under the apple trees and ten
minutes later you are married and living with her poor
old mother.

SECRETARY:

I am too young.

GENERAL:

Yes, and in a flash you'll be too old. You'll be sitting
at your desk dictating your memoirs. And between the
two, pouff—a game of dice. You must feel the urge
sometimes though, I hope?

SECRETARY:

No, sir. I have not long left the seminary. I am still
chaste.

GENERAL:

Good. Sad, though. Life without women, my boy, what hell! There's another problem M. Poincaré will never solve. Now then, to work. Where were we?

SECRETARY:

We have finished Chapter 30. Do you want me to read it back to you, sir?

GENERAL:

Not now. I'm feeling in form. I managed to slip out for ten minutes earlier on for a turn around the garden. The air was heavy with the scent of rhododendrons— I wandered down a path, it was cool, my joints were as sprightly as a two-year-old's—nobody called me—it was extraordinary. I fancied I was a widower. Chapter 31. My African Campaigns. Paragraph One. Morocco. Until 1898, the policy of the French Government in Morocco was a policy of presence. Since the ill-starred treaty of Frankfurt, however, another factor was coming to have a dangerous bearing on Moroccan policy; the creation of the German Empire whose intrigues and promises were to induce the Sultan to stiffen his attitude towards ourselves. An incident, to all appearances insignificant, was to set a light to the powder.

Enter ESTELLE *and* SIDONIA, *lanky wenches of rising twenty, still childish, ringletted, kiss-curled and wearing ridiculous little-girl dresses.*

SIDONIA:

Papa!

GENERAL:

Yes.

13]

SIDONIA:

What are we going to do about Corpus Christi?

GENERAL:

Nothing! We'll say we forgot.

ESTELLE:

But, Papa, Father Ambrose wants Sidonia and me in white, he said so again yesterday. And we have nothing to wear.

GENERAL:

Then wear nothing. It will be fifty times more jolly. Now then, my boy, where were we?

SECRETARY:

Relations between the Sultan and the government.

ESTELLE:

Papa! We are carrying the first banner in the procession directly behind the altarboys. We are your daughters and if we don't look as nice as all the other girls people will talk.

GENERAL:

People will talk anyway. Wear your last year's dresses!

SIDONIA:

They're too short. We've grown.

GENERAL:

Again? Hell's bells and little fishes, when are you going to stop? Look at me—have I grown?

ESTELLE:

People go on growing until the age of twenty-five.

[14

GENERAL:

They do in theory. But if they have a scrap of tact they leave off sooner. Go and put on your last year's dresses and come and show them to me.

GIRLS:

Yes, Papa!
> *They go.*

GENERAL:

> *Looking at them.*

My God, aren't they ugly? To think that I, with such a soft spot for a pretty face, could have brought those into the world.

SECRETARY:

The Mademoiselles Saint-Pé are full of all sorts of moral qualities.

GENERAL:

All sorts. But not the right sort. Heigh-ho—where were we?

SECRETARY:

Relations between the Sultan and the government.

GENERAL:

Well now, they weren't going so well either. One fine day the black bastard makes off with a couple of our missionaries. He has a bit of fun with them first and then sends them back, dead as pork, trussed up like sausages minus one or two spare parts. I won't dwell on the ironic element. It was an insult to the flag! The Dubreuil expedition is decided on! Ah, my boy, what a

15]

campaign! We got our money's worth for our two priests! By Jingo, we ran through some Arabs! With good clean steel too and no nonsense. And then, my boy, the little girls of twelve, the way they grow 'em in those parts—wonderful! There she is, terror-stricken, crouching naked in a corner, a little creature that knows it will be forced, and that desires it almost. Two young breasts, tender as fawns, and cruppers, me lad! And eyes!—and you the soldier, the conqueror, the master. Your sword still steaming in your hand—you have killed—you are all powerful—she knows it and you know it too—it is hot and dark inside the tent, and there you stand, face to face, in silence——

SECRETARY:

> *Flushed and panting.*

And then, sir?

GENERAL:

> *Simply.*

Well, dammit all—at that age! We're not savages. We turned them over to the Sisters of Mercy at Rabat.

> *Enter* DOCTOR BONFANT.

Ah! here's Dr. Bonfant come to see his patient. Leave us for a while, my boy.

> DOCTOR *and* SECRETARY *exchange "good mornings."*

I shall ring for you. Good morning, doctor.

> *The* SECRETARY *picks up his papers and leaves. The* GENERAL *watches him go.*

Fine-looking young chap, isn't he? Would have cut quite a dash as a dragoon but for his vocation as a

[16

virgin. Superb handwriting, though, and no fool. The Curé found him for me. He's a parish child one of his colleagues brought up.

DOCTOR:

And how is our invalid this morning?

GENERAL:

The same as yesterday, the same as tomorrow no doubt. And how is medical science progressing?

DOCTOR:

No further. We have found other terms far less vague than the old ones to designate the same complaints. It's a great advance linguistically. No scenes today?

GENERAL:

A small one on the usual theme. However, I took your advice and shut the door.

DOCTOR:

Excellent. And did that silence her?

GENERAL:

She must have gone on on the other side but at least I couldn't hear her.

DOCTOR:

As I say, this paralysis of the lower limbs is of a purely nervous origin, like all the rest. The mental process is quite simple—we won't walk any more so as to rouse his pity and make it impossible for him to leave us. You must have led her a dance to have brought her to that, General.

17]

GENERAL:

Not to that extent, Doctor, not to that extent. I loved my wife very much at first. Yes, it seems as odd to me now as my craze over a stamp collection at fifteen. But it's a fact, we had a few happy years—well, when I say happy. . . . Before lapsing into bigotry and fruit-bottling, Emily had quite an amorous disposition. My wife was an opera singer, you know. She bellowed her way through Wagner as a Valkyrie. I married her and made her give up the theatre, to my eternal cost. She was to go on acting for myself alone. A performance at his own expense, lasting for more than twenty years, tends to wear out your spectator. So I set about finding my fun elsewhere, naturally. Chambermaids, wait-resses, whatever hole-and-corner capers a man dares to indulge in, who is very closely watched. And I grew old, little by little. First a shade too much stomach, than the paunch advancing as the hair re-cedes, and the sleeve wound round with more and more gold string. And beneath this fancy dress the heart of an aged youngster still waiting for a chance to give his all. But who's to recognize me underneath the mask?

DOCTOR:

What would you say if I told you more or less the same tale, General?

GENERAL:

It wouldn't be the slightest consolation. At least your wife didn't decide at the eleventh hour to fall madly in love with you and die of unrequited passion.

[18

DOCTOR:

She makes up for it in other ways.
Rising.
Well now, I shall go and take her blood pressure. That won't do her any harm. It is always normal anyway. Does she eat at all?

GENERAL:

Like you or me. I shall make the most of your visit and take a little turn around the garden, like any carefree bachelor. Don't tell her, she would accuse me of deceiving her with a geranium.

> *The* DOCTOR *goes in to his patient, the* GENERAL *into the garden. The stage is empty for a moment. The* SECRETARY *is heard outside singing an Italian love song. The* MAID *shows in a visitor, a woman decked out in furs and feathers, and swathed in travelling veils.*

MAID:

It's very early, Madame. I think the master is taking his morning stroll around the garden.

MLLE. DE STE-EUVERTE:

Is that he singing? It sounds like his voice.

MAID:

Oh no, Madame. That's the Secretary. I'll go and ask the master if he will receive you, Madame.

MLLE. DE STE-E.:

Mademoiselle.

19]

MAID:

I beg your pardon, Mademoiselle. What name shall
I say?

MLLE. DE STE-E.:

Mlle. de Ste-Euverte.

MAID:

Very good, Mademoiselle.
The MAID *goes out.* MLLE. DE STE-EUVERTE
*makes a tour of the room, touching things
with her sunshade.*

MLLE. DE STE-E.:

Nothing has changed in this house.
She runs her finger along the table top.
Still as much dust as ever. The poor darling needs
someone badly.
She listens to the song and murmurs.
Strange—it sounds so like his voice.
The song stops. The GENERAL *appears in the
doorway, and stops, dumbfounded.*

GENERAL:

Ghislaine!

GHIS.:

Leon!

GENERAL:

You here?

GHIS.:

Yes. And with head held high.

[20

GENERAL:

There'll be the devil of a row.

GHIS.:

I came so that it might take place.

GENERAL:

> *Terrified.*

Careful. She's in that room.

GHIS.:

Alone?

GENERAL:

Doctor Bonfant is with her.

GHIS.:

I thought as much. I'll explain in a minute. First, let me look at you. Leon!

GENERAL:

Ghislaine! You!

GHIS.:

Myself.

GENERAL:

As intrepid as an Amazon!

GHIS.:

I took the night express. I found myself alone in the compartment with a fellow of sinister aspect who was pretending to read a newspaper.

GENERAL:

Anxiously.

Ghislaine. . . .

GHIS.:

At one point he asked me the time.

GENERAL:

The swine!

GHIS.:

But I gave him such a look that he took the hint immediately. He even said thank you as if I really had told him the time. He folded his newspaper and fell asleep. Or perhaps he was only pretending. But I was perfectly calm—I was armed. See, this little revolver with the mother-of-pearl handle which you may remember, Leon.

GENERAL:

Ghislaine, you have it still?

GHIS.:

Had he made one false move, had he so much as touched the hem of my dress I would have slain him first and myself afterwards—I had to get to you intact.

GENERAL:

Thank you, Ghislaine. But you know it's impossible, Ghislaine.

GHIS.:

Everything is possible, now. I have the proof of it here in my reticule. Our long years of waiting will not have been in vain, Leon.

GENERAL:

Seventeen years.

GHIS.:

Seventeen years since the Garrison Ball at Saumur.

GENERAL:

The Chinese lanterns, Ghislaine, the gypsy orchestra—
the colonel thought it too daring but I stood my
ground. They had been sent for all the way from Paris.

GHIS.:

Oh, the strange enchantment of that waltz, Leon!

GENERAL:

The Waltz of the Toreadors.

GHIS.:

Tra la la, la la la.

GENERAL:

Mademoiselle, may I have the pleasure?

GHIS.:

But, sir, you are not on my card.

GENERAL:

I will inscribe myself on it officially. Major St. Pé.
We have not been introduced but I feel that I have
known you all my life.

GHIS.:

Coyly.

Why, Major, how bold you are!—Then you took me
by the waist and all at once your hand burned me
right through your gloves and my dress. From the

23]

moment your hand touched my back I no longer heard the music. Everything whirled. . . .

GENERAL:

The waltz! Tra la la la—Tra la la——
> *He takes her in his arms and begins to waltz with her.*

GHIS.:

> *Swooning.*

It was love! Tra la la la——
> ESTELLE *and* SIDONIA *appear in the doorway in their over-short white dresses.*

SIDONIA:

Papa, we've come about the dresses.
> *The* GENERAL *hastily releases his partner.*

GENERAL:

Ten thousand demons, can't you see I'm busy? This lady is my teacher. I am having a dancing lesson.

ESTELLE:

Is there to be a ball then, Papa?

GENERAL:

> *Improvising wildly.*

I'm arranging one. For Corpus Christi funnily enough.
> *Introducing them.*

My daughters.

GHIS.:

Is it possible? Those darling little babies!

[24

GENERAL:

> *Shrugging.*

There we are!

GHIS.:

But it was only yesterday?

GENERAL:

They shot up very fast. You see, they've already grown out of their new dresses. This lady is an old friend who saw you when you were tiny. As for the dresses, it's clear you both want new ones. Granted. Run along to Mme. Dupont-Fredaine, choose the stuff . . .

ESTELLE:

Thank you, Papa!

SIDONIA:

Darling Papa!

GENERAL:

and tell her to come and see me about terms no later than this afternoon.

> *The GIRLS clap their hands.*

ESTELLE:

Oh, thank you, Papa!

SIDONIA:

We'll look lovely after all!

GENERAL:

Well, we'll have a shot at it anyhow.

> *The GIRLS skip out, hand in hand.*

GENERAL:

What a pair of silly geese! Heaven knows what tales they're going to spread.

GHIS.:

In a strangely altered voice.

But why are they so big? Leon, can I have aged as well?

GENERAL:

You are still the same Ghislaine, the same sweet tuber rose wafting her night-time fragrance over the gardens of Saumur!

GHIS.:

Wailing.

But I was eighteen years old at that ball!

GENERAL:

It never does to start adding up.

Taking her hand.

Your hand! Your little hand imprisoned in its glove. Do you remember that meringue at Rumpelmeyer's seven years ago?

GHIS.:

No. You're wrong. The whole of 1904 we couldn't meet at all. It was the beginning of her attacks. The meringue was 1903.

GENERAL:

I ate the little bits from off your fingers.

GHIS.:

You were as bold as brass even then. Yet we had only known each other a few years.

GENERAL:

Why count the years? It was a week ago. Your fingers still smell of meringue.

Enter the MAID.

[26

MAID:

Excuse me, sir.

GENERAL:

Starting.

Yes—what?

MAID:

The new one's come, sir.

GENERAL:

The new what?

MAID:

The new girl to replace Justine.

GENERAL:

Suffering catfish, can't you see I'm busy? I haven't time to go on choosing chambermaids. Engage her. . . .

On second thoughts.

What does she look like?

MAID:

A fine-looking girl, sir, dark and a little on the plump side.

GENERAL:

Dreamily.

A little on the plump side. . . . Engage her.

The MAID *goes out.*

GHIS.:

Leon, I wish you would let me help you. You don't know what you may be getting.

GENERAL:

Thank you, Ghislaine, but there's no need. From what I hear she's sure to be very nice. Besides, we have

27]

decisions to make. Your presence here is unthinkable, my love, you know that.

GHIS.:

This time, though, I am quite determined to stay.

GENERAL:

What did you say?

GHIS.:

Solemnly.

Leon, I have waited for so long in silence, keeping myself for you. If I were to bring you positive proof of the unworthiness of her for whom we sacrificed ourselves, what would you do?

GENERAL:

Unworthiness? Emily unworthy? Alas, Ghislaine, you must be dreaming.

GHIS.:

Yes, Leon, I am dreaming, dreaming that I am about to live at last! In this reticule I hold clasped to my heart I have two letters. Two letters signed by her hand. Two love letters to a man.

GENERAL:

Thundering cannonballs, it can't be true!

GHIS.:

On his bosom.

We are free, Leon!

GENERAL:

Who is it? I demand to know his name!

GHIS.:
> Doctor Bonfant.

GENERAL:
> Doctor Bonfant!
>> *The* DOCTOR *enters, beaming.*

DOCTOR:
> General, I am happy to be able to tell you that she is much better today. We chatted for a while and that appeared to soothe her. You see how wrong you are to poke fun at doctoring. It all depends on the doctor, and the way one goes about it.

GENERAL:
>> *Icily.*
> No need to labor the point, sir. There is a young lady present.
>> *The* DOCTOR *turns to* MLLE. DE STE-EUVERTE *in mild surprise.*

DOCTOR:
> I do beg your pardon.
>> *Bowing.*
> Madame.

GHIS.:
>> *With infinite nobility.*
> Mademoiselle. But not for very long now!

>> *The* DOCTOR *straightens, astonished.*

>> ***Black Out***

ACT ONE

SCENE TWO

The same. The GENERAL *and the* DOCTOR *are alone. The latter seated, the* GENERAL *pacing feverishly about the room.*

GENERAL:

What do you say to swords, sir?

DOCTOR:

General, I say you are quite wrong.

GENERAL:

Blood must be shed, sir! I shall listen to your explanations afterwards.

DOCTOR:

It may be a trifle late by then.

GENERAL:

I can't help that. Blood to begin with, sir!

DOCTOR:

You're quite right. With the present state of your arteries . . . How about a little cut with the lancet first? I have my bag here.

GENERAL:

Your sawbones humor is uncalled for, sir.

[30

DOCTOR:

I am quite serious. Blood pressure is our triumph. It is one of the few chances we have of being accurate, thanks to our little gadget here. That is why we take it on every conceivable occasion. The last time you were up to two hundred and fifty. That's very high, you know.

GENERAL:

I don't care, sir. I shall consult one of your colleagues. It is a question of honor at the moment.
After a pause.
Two hundred and fifty, is that high?

DOCTOR:

Very.

GENERAL:

After another slight pause.
Did you or did you not receive those letters?

DOCTOR:

I tell you I never did. If I had, how could they come to be in your possession?

GENERAL:

True enough. . . . You've seen them, though. They aren't forgeries.

DOCTOR:

Apparently not.

31]

GENERAL:

Therefore, sir, the fact is this: my wife is in love with you.

DOCTOR:

So she writes.

GENERAL:

And you consider that perfectly normal, do you?

DOCTOR:

What can I do about it?

GENERAL:

By Jove, sir, has the Medical Corps no honor! Any cadet—what am I saying?—any regular N.C.O. would already have replied—at your service! Explanations would have followed later. How would you like it if I slapped your face?

DOCTOR:

I should promptly slap yours back, sir. And there I should have the advantage of you. I am Acting President of the sports club of which you are merely the Honorary Secretary. I do an hour's training every morning. You spoke about your paunch just now. We are the same age. Just look at mine.

GENERAL:

Grudgingly.
You're pulling it in.

DOCTOR:

No. Feel it, it's quite natural. Now look at yours.
The GENERAL undoes his own trousers and examines his figure.

[32

GENERAL:

Holy Moses!

DOCTOR:

Go on, feel. Feel mine. Now feel yours.

> MLLE. DE STE-EUVERTE *appears in the doorway of the morning room.*

M. DE STE-E.:

Oh, my God, you're wounded!

> *The* DOCTOR *and the* GENERAL *hastily pull up their trousers.*

GENERAL:

No, no, of course not. Go back into the morning room, and don't come out whatever you do. We will call you when it's all over.

> *He propels her into the morning room and sits down defeated, beside the* DOCTOR, *completing the adjustments to his dress.*

What a business!

DOCTOR:

I am all at sea, I must confess. Who is this young woman?

GENERAL:

Young girl, sir, a friend of mine. I forbid you to jump to any conclusions.

DOCTOR:

If I cannot even form a supposition I shall be more at sea than ever.

GENERAL:

Mlle. de Ste-Euverte—a lady descended from one of the noblest houses of Lorraine—is the love of my life, Doctor, and I am hers. I met her at the annual Ball of the Eighth Dragoons at Saumur in 1893, seventeen years ago. She was a girl of the best society, I was a married man. Anything between us was quite out of the question. At the time, owing to my career and the children, I dared not contemplate divorce. And yet we could not give up our love. Seventeen years that's been going on! Mlle. de Ste-Euverte is still a maiden and I am still a prisoner.

DOCTOR:

But dammit, General, your career is established, your daughters are grown up, what in Heaven are you waiting for?

GENERAL:

I'll tell you a secret, Doctor, a miserable secret. I am a coward.

DOCTOR:

Stuff and nonsense, General. You wanted to run me through a minute ago. And what about your oak-leaves and your eighteen wounds?

GENERAL:

Simply.
Those were done to me. It's not the same. Besides, in battle it's comparatively simple. Life is a different thing.
A pause. He says dully.
I can't make people suffer.

[34

DOCTOR:

Gently.

Then you will make them suffer a great deal, my friend, and you will suffer a great deal yourself.

GENERAL:

I fear so.

DOCTOR:

Let us sum up the situation, shall we? I want to help you out of this dilemma. You are in love with this young woman.

GENERAL:

Young girl, sir.

DOCTOR:

Young girl, if you prefer it. She loves you. She has spent years waiting for you. She sacrificed her youth in vain anticipation of a happiness which you once promised her. You owe her that happiness now.

GENERAL:

I know. Not a minute has gone by during those seventeen years that has not been poisoned by the thought of it. What is she doing? She is alone, playing the piano in the deserted drawing room of her big house, doing her embroidery, eating alone at her vast table in the chilly dining room where my place is always laid and always vacant. I know it, sir, I know it all. Time and again I have seized my service revolver—I'm not afraid of death—he's an old comrade—bang-bang, all over. For me, not for her. I had no right to do it.

35]

DOCTOR:

Leave your revolver, like your sword, up on the wall, General. Among all your military equipment did you never think of your kitbag?

GENERAL:

My kitbag?

DOCTOR:

Two shirts, three pairs of pants, six handkerchiefs, hey presto! and Mlle. de Ste-Euverte is no longer —a young girl!

GENERAL:

And my wife, sir?

DOCTOR:

Do you love her?

GENERAL:

Lord, no. But she loves me. She'll die of it.

DOCTOR:

Hum, I wonder. Women have unexpected reserves. I understand she wrote to say she was in love with me.

GENERAL:

Leaping up.

Upon my soul, sir, how dare you! You have offended me! To the sword, sir! To the sword!

DOCTOR:

Now, General, we must try to understand each other. If you kill a man for her sake, I can't see you anywhere near to leaving her. You must be logical, General.

[36

GENERAL:

Can you swear that you are not her lover?

DOCTOR:

On the head of Mme. Bonfant.

GENERAL:

Anyway she's ugly—nothing but a bag of bones.

DOCTOR:

Oh no, General. Your wife was never what one would call a beauty, but when you came to live here fifteen years ago, I don't mind telling you, my dear fellow, that she created quite a stir. Not in me, sir, not in me, particularly! But her personality, her clothes, her talent.... Very attractive woman, sir, was your wife, and then, coming from Paris as she did....

GENERAL:

She comes from Carpentras.

DOCTOR:

She had just come from Paris nonetheless, and from the Opera. You know what they are in the provinces. I am personally acquainted with two who at all events nursed secret hopes.

GENERAL:

Awful in his anger.
Their names!

DOCTOR:

What is the use, General, now? One of them is in a wheel chair through sacrificing overmuch to Venus. The other is dead.

37]

GENERAL:

Always too late.

DOCTOR:

Exactly. The more I think of it, General, the more I am disturbed by your case. This constant living in the past.

GENERAL:

I know. I forget my paunch and the gold strings on my sleeve. I am old.

DOCTOR:

Your jealousy of Mme. St. Pé was fine in the old tooth-and-nail days. What can it possibly matter to you now? Your love for Mlle. de Ste-Euverte was for Mlle. de Ste-Euverte as a young girl the night of the Garrison Ball. That one has been dead these many years. Neither you nor she herself can so much as recall what she once was.

GENERAL:

With a disarming smile.

Oh, yes, Doctor, dear me, yes!

DOCTOR:

A tender memory. The memory of a dead girl. And Major St. Pé is dead too. Turn your attention to your rose trees. You haven't so much longer, you know. Why not forget him?

GENERAL:

Never! The heart has stayed the same, sir, under the ironmongery!

Springing to attention.

Lieutenant St. Pé! Graduated second from Saumur!

[38

No money, but plenty of courage and well thought of!
Ready to give his all for France, for honor, for a
woman! A real woman, sweet and loving and faithful
and pure; not that third-rate prima donna! I am thirty
years old! I swear I am! And I did find that woman. I
found her last night, at the Annual Ball at Saumur.
I am ready.

DOCTOR:

Then you must make haste, General. One good honest
explanation. Cut to the quick before gangrene sets in.
Hurt if you must but do it without flinching. And
then start again afresh. Crossing the threshold of that
door seems like flying to the moon, but in fact all it
requires is this one step.

> GHISLAINE *appears at the door.*

GHIS.:

I can't stand it! I must know!

GENERAL:

> *Slightly on edge.*

Dammit all, Ghislaine, you've waited seventeen years,
surely you can contain yourself for an extra ten
minutes.

GHIS.:

No I can't, not even for ten minutes.

GENERAL:

I must have time enough to make her confess, and
inform her of my irrevocable decision. She is an invalid,

39]

dammit. I owe her consideration. Don't you be cruel, too.

GHIS.:

I bore her cruelty and respected her love so long as I believed her faithful to you. Now I know that she dared to betray you I shall know no pity, Leon, and no patience. Either way, should you be capable of hesitating still, I have a little revolver with a mother-of-pearl handle which you may remember, here in my reticule. I shall end this life within the hour, without ever having known more of love than your vain promises, Leon.

GENERAL:

Give me strength! All I ask is a moment to set my life in order. Go back into the morning room and be patient. There are some magazines on the table.

GHIS.:

Magazines! Like at the dentist's! You have wounded me for the first time, my dear.

GENERAL:

My beloved! Who said anything about a dentist? Anyhow, you aren't the one who is going to have the tooth out. Just one moment.

> *He pushes her gently but firmly back into the morning room.*

I adore you!

DOCTOR:

General!

> *Points to bedroom.*

[40

GENERAL:

Time is getting on. Suppose you spoke to her first, Doctor?

DOCTOR:

That might prove a little awkward considering those letters. Suppose she falls into my arms? There'll be no end of explaining to do then.

GENERAL:

That's true. Stay here, though, will you, and if I shout "Help", come in.

> *He goes into his wife's room, and rushes out again almost at once, distractedly waving a letter.*

Doctor, she's not in her room!

DOCTOR:

What! Is there another way out?

GENERAL:

Through the window, by hanging on to the wisteria.

DOCTOR:

In her condition——

GENERAL:

She left this letter on the table. "I heard everything. Men are all cowards. Whatever they may have said to you, Leon, I have never loved anyone but you. I can walk when I want to. I am going. You will never hear of me again." Does she mean she wants to kill herself?

41]

DOCTOR:

Looking at his watch.

The railroad crossing! She spoke of it! The train goes through at five past! It's two minutes to!

GENERAL:

The pond! You go one way—I'll go the other!

They both rush out. GHISLAINE *comes in almost at once.*

GHIS.:

I too heard everything. You love her still, Leon! Only one way out.

She sits at the desk and begins to write rapidly, calm but dabbing away a tear through her veil.

Murmuring.

Leon, here is my last letter to you . . .

Her voice trails away, she continues to write. GASTON, *the* SECRETARY, *is heard outside the window, singing his Italian love song. The ditty continues throughout the writing of the letter. When she has finished,* GHISLAINE *leaves it on the General's desk in a prominent position.*

GHIS.:

There. On his books. That's all. It's the simplest thing in the world.

She rises unhurriedly, picks up her reticule, draws out the revolver with the mother-of-pearl handle, presses it to her heart, and

pulls the trigger. Nothing happens. She looks at the gun in surprise, pulls out a catch, pushes another, blows into the barrel, and fires again. Still nothing.
Sighing.

You too have been waiting seventeen years.

She throws away the gun, looks at her fobwatch and mutters.

Too late for the train. The pond!

She runs to the door, but changes her mind.

No. Not in the same place as her, for Heaven's sake!

She darts a quick look round the room.

The window! With a little luck. . . .

She takes a run at it, swings her legs over the balcony and drops. The singing ends abruptly in a loud hiccup. The stage is empty for a moment. MAID *ad libs off stage.*

MAID:

For goodness sakes—what was that? Who screamed that way? What's the matter—what happened—someone go fetch the Master quickly.

Then GASTON *enters carrying a senseless* GHISLAINE, *closely followed by the* MAID.

MAID:

Goodness gracious, sir, whatever's the matter? You yelled fit to raise the dead!

GASTON:

I was rocking quietly in the hammock when this lady comes tumbling down on my head.

43]

MAID:

Well, fancy that! Maybe she wanted to kill you?

GASTON:

Herself more likely. Besides I don't know her from Adam. She's fainted.
He puts her down on the couch.

MAID:

And the doctor just this minute left. The man as good as lives here half the time, and the one day we have a suicide he's out.

GASTON:

Slapping GHISLAINE's *face.*
For God's sake go and fetch something.

MAID:

What?

GASTON:

Well, *I* don't know—ointment, smelling salts—iodine. . . . Anything!

MAID:

I'll make her a good strong cup of coffee.
She goes.

GASTON:

No blood anyway.
He feels her all over.
No bones broken, apparently. No bumps. Madame! Madame!

[44

GHIS.:

> *Weakly.*

Mademoiselle.

GASTON:

Mademoiselle—I beg your pardon. Are you feeling better?

GHIS.:

> *Murmuring.*

Leave your hands where they are, Leon.

GASTON:

> *Turning away in embarrassment.*

Excuse me, but you are making a mistake.

GHIS.:

> *Crying out.*

Leave your hands, Leon—caressing me—or I feel I shall swoon again—your hands quickly—I'm going——

GASTON:

> *Looking in panic at his hands.*

My hands? Oh, dear, I can't very well let her faint away again. Not that it's at all unpleasant, and I am such a lonely young man. Besides, I'll mention it when I go to confession.

GHIS.:

Oh, how good it feels! You are touching me at last, Leon! You thought me strong—and I was strong, I had to be, but oh, how long they were, all those nights on my own! Before I met you I was alone too, but I never knew it. It was on the morrow of the Saumur Ball that my bed suddenly seemed wide. That next night and all the nights for seventeen years. And all the wicked thoughts—you don't know! I shall never tell you. I struggled alone. No one was to touch me until you finally came. Your arms are strong and gentle your hands, gentler even than at the Saumur Ball. Kiss me, now that you know I am going to die. What are you waiting for, Leon, my death!

GASTON:

The lady is obviously making a mistake, but seeing that she may be going to die——
He kisses her.

GHIS.:

Has the time to sigh.

At last!

A long kiss. Enter the GENERAL, *carrying his unconscious* WIFE *in his arms. He stands rooted to the spot at the sight which confronts him.*

GENERAL:

What the devil do you think you're doing?

GASTON:

Getting to his feet in terror.
But, sir, the lady is delirious.

GENERAL:

Bawling.
Fifty thousand devils, I can well believe it!

GASTON:

She fell on top of me, sir, and ordered me to kiss her.

[46

GENERAL:

Hell's bells, has everyone round here gone mad this morning?

> *Still encumbered with his unconscious* WIFE, *shouting.*

What's wrong with you? What happened?

GASTON:

She threw herself out of the window, sir. Thank goodness I was underneath in the hammock. She landed right on my head.

GENERAL:

Out of the window! Holy Moses, they're insane, the lot of them! My beloved! Here, my boy, take my wife will you?

> *He puts his* WIFE *into* GASTON'S *arms and throws himself down beside* GHISLAINE.

Ghislaine! My dearest! Why did you want to die?

GHIS.:

> *Coming to.*

Who is that touching me? I do not know those hands!

GENERAL:

It's I, Ghislaine—Leon. Your Leon.

GHIS.:

> *Pushing him away.*

Let me go. You aren't Leon. I don't recognize your hands.

> *The* GENERAL *kisses her.*

Nor your mouth. Leon kissed me just now, at long

47]

last. He is twenty years old. I forbid you to touch me. No one may touch me but him. I am keeping myself.

GENERAL'S WIFE:

Coming to in the SECRETARY'S *arms.*

Leon!

GENERAL:

Picking up GHISLAINE.

That's done it. The other one will come to in a minute. She mustn't see her here. She'd kill herself a second time.

WIFE:

Clinging to the SECRETARY'S *neck and screeching.*

Leon, hold me! Kiss me, Leon! You can see I'm dying. Kiss me quickly before I am quite dead!

SECRETARY:

Yelling in his panic after the GENERAL *who is carrying* GHISLAINE *away.*

This one wants to be kissed before she dies as well!!! What am I to do?

GENERAL:

You must be out of your mind, my boy! Can't you see they're both delirious? Put Madame down in her room. I am taking this young lady in here.

They both go out with their unconscious burdens. The MAID *comes in with the coffee.*

Curtain

[48

ACT TWO

ACT TWO

SCENE ONE

The same. The GENERAL *is alone. He appears to be waiting. The* DOCTOR *comes out of the morning room.*

GENERAL:

Well?

DOCTOR:

They are both resting. I gave them a good sedative. The snag is that they will eventually wake up.

GENERAL:

We are so peaceful as we are! It's most odd, for an hour now there hasn't been a sound. I was even on the point of gathering a few ideas. You know, science ought to find a way of putting women permanently to sleep. We could wake them for a while at night and then they would go back to sleep again.

DOCTOR:

But what about the housework? You should see the performance I have to fry myself an egg—and that's nothing, there's the washing up afterwards!

51]

GENERAL:

If the worst came to the worst we wouldn't put the maids to sleep. Have you seen the latest little one? With all these upsets I haven't even had a chance to say hullo to her. A bosom, my dear chap!

Sighing.

Dear Lord, how simple it could all be! Why do we complicate life so?

DOCTOR:

Because we have a soul, General. Take an old free-thinker's word for it. It's that which makes life hell for us. The maid's petticoats are pleasant at times, but afterwards—without love, without any real desire— what emptiness! I'll tell you a secret, General. We have all stayed little boys. Only the little girls grow up.

GENERAL:

Suddenly.

There is one though, who never hurt me, who never once complained. True, I never lived with her. Oh, if you could have seen her at the Saumur Ball! I bet you don't believe that I really love her, having waited all this time?

DOCTOR:

My dear man, one must never judge the courage or the love of others. No one can say who loves or is afraid.

GENERAL:

There's my life story, Doctor, in a nutshell. The shell is handsome. They have painted the oakleaves onto it, and Lord knows how many decorations. I have a lovely

[52

house, splendid whiskers, the easy wenches in these parts refuse me nothing. When I go by on my black mare of a morning, in my corsets, I'll even wager I make the little virgins at the High School that peep behind their curtains dream of me. I utter enormities when the fancy takes me, and everyone turns a deaf ear, even the priest, because I have a way with me. Well, my friend, the shell is empty. There's nobody inside. I am alone, and I'm afraid.

DOCTOR:

Afraid of what?

GENERAL:

I dunno. Of my loneliness, I suppose.

DOCTOR:

My poor old friend.

GENERAL:

My bits of fun, even, do you think they amuse me? They bore me to death. It is my terror of living which sends me scampering after them. When you see them swinging by with their buttocks and their breasts under their dresses you feel I don't know what wild hope surge up inside you! But once the dress is off and you have to get down to it! The only thing is that with all these philanderings you get to my age realizing that you have never in your life made love. It's wrong of me to make fun of my secretary. I am an old virgin, Doctor.

DOCTOR:

No. You have the sickness, General, that's all.

53]

GENERAL:

Which one? I've had them all.

DOCTOR:

Those sicknesses are nothing. They can be treated. We have a soul, General. I long denied the phenomenon. I was one of the old school. We did not bother with that subject in my day. I wanted to stick to abscesses and cancers. But now I know. It's in the soul the trouble lies, in nine cases out of ten.

GENERAL:

But dammit all, everybody has a soul! That's no reason for being scared out of one's wits a whole life long.

DOCTOR:

It is, General. Souls are rare. And when by ill luck you happen to possess one, it's war if you don't make your peace with it.

GENERAL:

Peace, peace? But what brand of peace does it want, damn its eyes? It surely doesn't expect me to take Holy Orders, does it?

DOCTOR:

No. If it were as simple as that you would have done it long ago.

GENERAL:

Then what *does* the jade want? The only time I feel slightly at peace is when I look at something beautiful. Dammit, I can't turn myself into a painter or sculptor, can I? What then? Scuttling from art gallery to museum like a half-wit, brandishing a Kodak? No, by heaven! Beauty's a thing one should be able to fashion for oneself.

DOCTOR:

What about Mlle. de Ste-Euverte, General?

GENERAL:

After a pause.

Well, yes, there it is. You know, it's an extraordinary thing what happened to me at Saumur—there was a girl—like any other—the color of her dress and hair had caught my eye—I introduce myself, ask her for the dance. The Waltz of the Toreadors. Tra-la— Take her by the waist and I say to myself—how good I feel! What's happening to me? I have suddenly ceased to be afraid. It was an enchanted moment, Doctor.

DOCTOR:

And did it happen again?

GENERAL:

Every time. At all our pathetic little meetings. Each time came the miracle. I suddenly stopped being afraid.

DOCTOR:

Why in heaven's name did you wait so long?

GENERAL:

It's easy to talk. You don't know the old bitch—I mean my soul. When she is face to face with my wife, she bawls with disgust and fright; but when I make Emily cry, when she starts to whimper in her wheel-chair, where I know she only sits in order to annoy

55]

me—when I am at last about to throttle her—don't
laugh, it has crossed my mind—and take my cap off
the hallstand to decamp once and for all, do you know
what she does then, the great goop?—My soul, that
is—? She cuts off my legs, she floods me with pity,
mean ignoble pity, and old memories of love from the
days when everything was not dried up and stale between us. She roots me to the spot. So then I hang
my hat back on the peg again. And I take my soul on
a little jaunt to the brothel, to see if it won't cheer her
up a bit. Have you got a soul, Doctor?

DOCTOR:

Yes, but she's extremely shy and fairly modest in her
demands.

GENERAL:

Well, don't let her get out of hand. Rule her with a
rod of iron, for if you don't she'll have your skin!
> *He stands by the door of the morning room.*
> *Murmuring dreamily.*

Dear Ghislaine! Dear, sweet, patient Ghislaine! Dear
little soldier on half pay! Dear widow!
> *Turning to the* DOCTOR.

Give her a little less gardenal than the other one, will
you? I should so like to console her.

DOCTOR:
> *Smiling.*

Very well. I am very fond of you, General. And to
think we were within an ace of murdering each other
over that letter business!

[56

GENERAL:

Thumping his breast with clenched fist.

God in heaven, what a fool I am! Suppose I thought of myself a little for a change! Me! Me! I exist too, don't I? Suppose I gave up trying to understand others for a minute? How good it would be! What do you say, Doctor?

DOCTOR:

The best thing you could do, General, if you can bring yourself to do it.

GENERAL:

Then it's all settled. Inspection over. Dis-miss! Carry on!

Enter the SECRETARY.

Ah, there you are, my boy. You're in luck. I'm in a rollicking mood. We are going to mop up the chapter on Morocco in two shakes of a lamb's tail, and we'll postpone the next one until ten years from now. I'll show them what stuff I'm made of!

DOCTOR:

I'll leave you, General. My wife is going to think I'm here a bit too often. I don't have to tell you what reproaches are, eh? I shall look in to see them both this evening. You should take advantage of the sedative to rehearse your lines for the big scene.

GENERAL:

I'm bearing them in mind. But it's so good to talk of something else for a minute. I shall take a little stroll around Morocco and come straight home again.

The DOCTOR *goes.*

57]

Now, let's get back to our two sky pilots. As I was saying, there they were, with some parts missing. Write down: A fearful mutilation, the details of which one hesitates to enlarge upon, perpetrated on the persons of two saintly churchmen, placed us under the sorry obligation of shedding blood ourselves.

> *Enter* ESTELLE *and* SIDONIA, *followed by* MME. DUPONT-FREDAINE, *a mighty handsome dressmaker.*

SIDONIA:

Papa, we've come about the dresses.

GENERAL:

Will you leave me in peace? I've other fish to fry just now. We go into the attack first thing in the morning.

MME. D.-F.:

General!

GENERAL:

> *Seeing her.*

Why, Mme. Dupont-Fredaine! I'm delighted to see you. Lovely and tempting and swish-swishing as ever!

> *Kissing her hand.*

By Jove, what a figure! What allure! Mme. Dupont-Fredaine, you are the loveliest woman in the neighborhood.

MME. D.-F.:

Now, General, that's all over and done with. We must think of the young ones now. You gave us very little notice, you know—we had to perform miracles to make beauties out of these two girlies.

GENERAL:

Miracles, how right you are.

MME. D.-F.:

Giving him a little slap.
What do you say to this little frill at the bottom, hinted at again in the sleeves? I think it's a dream!

GENERAL:

Enchanting! Enchanting! Your own dress is delightful, too. What is this splendid material?

MME. D.-F.:

Warding off the gesture.
General! Look at your daughters. Their material is very much more beautiful.

GENERAL:

Vaguely.
Lovely, lovely! Is it going to cost a lot?

MME. D.-F.:

Now, General, you know I'm very reasonable——

GENERAL:

Close to her.
Oh, Emma, how I wish you were!

MME. D.-F.:

Now, now. Let's not talk about the price. The young ladies wanted to make sure of pleasing you, and M. Gaston, too, I fancy!

SECRETARY:
> *Blushing.*
> But Madame, I am not qualified to judge. I have so little experience of young ladies.

MME. D.-F.:
> When one is twenty years of age and handsome one is always qualified, young man. Why, he's blushing! He's adorable, this secretary of yours, General!

GENERAL:
> Ten thousand demons, Madame, I forbid you to adore him!

MME. D.-F.:
> Walk around the room, will you, young ladies? The gentlemen will give us their verdict.
> *While the girls are parading, the* GENERAL *approaches* MME. D.-F.

GENERAL:
> These repeated refusals are absurd, you know, Emma.

MME. D.-F.:
> Stop it now. You are a wicked old wolf. My husband is a friend of yours.

GENERAL:
> Exactly. Nobody would take the least exception. Charming! Charming! I really must have a serious talk with you about the cost of these fal-lals, dear lady! Do come for a little stroll around the garden, won't you? I shall present you with a rose. We won't be a

[60

moment, girls. Gaston, I leave them in your care, my boy.

> *He goes out with the* DRESSMAKER. *The two* GIRLS *hurl themselves onto* GASTON.

SIDONIA:

Aren't you ashamed, letting her say you're adorable?

ESTELLE:

An old fly-by-night like her! Doesn't it matter to you that we are pining away?

SECRETARY:

But, my dear young ladies, how could I help it?

ESTELLE:

And the other one this morning, I suppose you couldn't help her either? Why did you kiss her?

SIDONIA:

It's shameful. Everybody saw you.

SECRETARY:

I was alone.

ESTELLE:

You don't think we ever leave you alone, do you? We never let you out of our sight. We were ouside on the stairs.

SECRETARY:

She had fallen on top of me. She was dying. What else could I do?

ESTELLE:

You swore, Gaston.

61]

SIDONIA:

You swore, one or the other.

SECRETARY:

I love you both, young ladies.

ESTELLE:

Yet it's a third you kiss. A nice thing!

SIDONIA:

Ah, my dear—men! Does it surprise you? What a little child you are!

ESTELLE:

You never even kiss us!

SECRETARY:

But you are young ladies. Besides, there are always two of you.

The girls turn to each other in fury.

SIDONIA:

Ooh!

ESTELLE:

You see!

SIDONIA:

You see!

ESTELLE:

You never let me see him alone!

SIDONIA:

No, it's you!

ESTELLE:

'Tisn't! It's you!

[62

SIDONIA:

'Tisn't! It's you! You pudding!

ESTELLE:

You skinny lizard!

SIDONIA:

You old bag of lard! You soppy sausage you!

ESTELLE:

You string bean!
> *They fight. The* SECRETARY, *distracted, hops ineffectually around trying to separate them.*

SECRETARY:

Ladies! Ladies! Help! Help! Oh, my goodness, they'll murder each other!
> MME. DUPONT-FREDAINE *and the* GENERAL, *very red in the face, come flying in.*

MME. D.-F.:

Young ladies! Your dresses!

GENERAL:
> *Shouting.*

Holy suffering catfish, have you finished? Where did I get such a pair of misbegotten frumps? What is going on? Explain yourselves!

SIDONIA:

She started it!

ESTELLE:

I didn't! She did!

63]

GENERAL:
Devil take it, man, I leave them in your charge and you can't even stop them fighting!

MME. D.-F.:
On her knees repairing the damage.
Oh, your dresses! Your dresses! Little vandals!

GENERAL:
Answer me! What were they fighting about?

SECRETARY:
Crimson.
I can't tell you, sir.

GENERAL:
Can't tell me, eh? Ye gods and little fishes, who is making a monkey out of who? You two, come here! What were you fighting about?
No answer.

ESTELLE:
Blurting it out.
Papa! We love him to distraction!

SIDONIA:
Both of us!

GENERAL:
Whom?

ESTELLE: ⎫
SIDONIA: ⎭ *Sobbing.*
Him!
[64

GENERAL:

That is the rampaging limit!

ESTELLE:

But, Papa, you don't know what it's like to be in love!

MME. D.-F.:

Ladies! Ladies! You're weeping onto your dresses!

GENERAL:

Blood and giblets, that's a good one! That emasculated virgin?

MME. D.-F.:

General!

GENERAL:

Sorry, it slipped out. That zany? That trashy little penpusher?

ESTELLE:

Papa, what's emasculated?

GENERAL:

Jumping Jehosophat, leave the room this instant! Be so good as to take them away, Mme. Dupont-Fredaine, and leave me with this young bumpkin here. I don't know what's going on in this house, but things are beginning to get out of hand.

MME. D.-F.:

It's love, General!

GENERAL:

That's rich! Love isn't an excuse for everything.

65]

MME. D.-F.:

> *Giving him a surreptitious little slap on her way out.*

Naughty fibber! You just told me the very opposite! Goodbye for the moment.

GENERAL:

> *Winking.*

See you later, Emma.

> *The* WOMEN *go out.*

Well, what have you got to say for yourself, sir?

SECRETARY:

I don't know, sir. I am quite overcome.

GENERAL:

Exactly! You were recommended to me by a venerable ecclesiastic who vouched for your morals and your handwriting. I had up till now testified to the excellence of both.

SECRETARY:

I swear to you that nothing in my behavior could have incited the young ladies to——

GENERAL:

Don't drown the salmon, sir! Nothing in your behavior could have incited you to kiss Mlle. de Ste-Euverte on the mouth this morning either, I suppose?

SECRETARY:

She mistook me for someone else, sir.

GENERAL:

That makes it even worse! You are an imposter, sir!

[66

SECRETARY:

No, General! But the terrifying thing is that while I held her in my arms I quite thought that it was me she loved.

GENERAL:

She wasn't properly conscious, my boy.

SECRETARY:

Bitterly.
She kept calling me Leon.

GENERAL:

Easily.
Leon? What a coincidence! The name of her intended, no doubt?

SECRETARY:

But all the same it was to me she said it.

GENERAL:

Bursting out laughing.
Ha ha, that's a good one! That's very good! So you think one falls in love like that, do you? At first sight and for always? Fiddlesticks! You must gorge yourself on cheap novels!

SECRETARY:

No, sir, on the classics, exclusively. But the course of events is frequently quite similar.
With dignity.
In any case I intend to confess to this lady when she is once more herself, and offer to make amends.

67]

GENERAL:

Confess? Confess what? You will do no such thing. I will not have you confuse the wits of this unfortunate girl. Am I going to have to teach you, by roundly boxing your ears, just what a young girl's honor means? I've seen you already, my lad, with that last little maid we had here. Don't deny it! I tell you I saw you!

SECRETARY:

It was she who pursued me, sir. I avoided her. She was always coming up behind me in the passages——

GENERAL:

Oh, the little bitch!

SECRETARY:

She said she was fed to the teeth with this dump—I quote, of course—and that she absolutely had to have a young one.

GENERAL:

Interrupting in a voice of thunder.

Young man! You are on the threshold of life, but you appear to me to be totally devoid of principles. You were put into my care—I could be your father—and it is my duty to instill those principles into you. Hold your tongue! You will speak when your turn comes and not before. Sit down! Firstly, one point about which it is forbidden to make light. Honor. Do you know what I mean by honor?

SECRETARY:

Yes, sir.

[68

GENERAL:

I should hope so. You have been bred on the classics, you say? I do not therefore have to teach you the fable of that Spartan youth who, having stolen a fox and hidden it beneath his tunic, preferred to have his stomach gnawed away sooner than confess his theft? This admirable fable contains a moral. Will you kindly tell me what that moral is?

SECRETARY:

After a moment's hesitation.

Never confess.

GENERAL:

No, sir, wrong answer.

SECRETARY:

Never steal a fox.

GENERAL:

Wrong again. He did steal. But having stolen, what remained for our young Spartan to do then?

SECRETARY:

Give back the fox and take his punishment.

GENERAL:

No, sir. In allowing his stomach to be gnawed away without a murmur he did better. He showed that he had honor. Draw the moral, now that I have put you on the right track.

SECRETARY:

When one does something contrary to honor, honor consists in never owning up to it.

69]

GENERAL:

No, sir! That is pride which is an insufferable fault.

SECRETARY:

I give up, sir.

GENERAL:

Ha! You give up, do you? Do you indeed? I can see your sense of honor is choking you! A nice bunch I must say, the younger generation! If the War Office is counting on your sort to hoist the flag. . . . However, the meaning of this fable, sir, is very simple. Honor bids me not to steal. Right, I do steal—unless one is a born idiot one sidesteps the rules and regulations now and then. But, one thing is certain, I am not capable of forfeiting my honor. Therein lies the principle. I have been caught. Therein lies the accident. Never let yourself be caught. Am I, a young Spartan, going to be found wanting in honor? No. I cannot be found wanting in honor. Hence there is no fox under my tunic. You get it?

SECRETARY:

No, sir.

GENERAL:

Never mind. You'll understand when you grow up. Simply retain from all this that it is essential to keep up appearances. Let us take a more familiar instance. You are sleeping with the maid.

SECRETARY:

Shocked.

General!

[70

GENERAL:

Don't have a fit. You were on the verge of doing so, you young Pecksniff. And if you weren't a born ass you would have. To resume, honor is strong, but the flesh is weak. You are hot blooded. You've got the wench under your skin—when she brushes past you in the passage, something goes *Bmp* in your stomach. Do you for all that pinch her bottom at table in the middle of luncheon?

SECRETARY:

Blushing at the suggestion.
Oh no, sir.

GENERAL:

No, you simply say, "Leontine, please bring us some bread." And yet you know perfectly well it isn't a bread roll you're after. Luncheon runs its course, impeccably, does it not?

SECRETARY:

Yes, sir.

GENERAL:

Life, Gaston, is one long family lunch, tiresome because it has to be performed according to a long-established ritual, with initialed napkin rings, embroidered table mats, forks of different shapes and sizes and a bell push under the table. It is a game we have agreed to play. So we have to play according to the rules; answer the children's questions, divide the plum tart into equal slices, scold the youngest when he dribbles, fold one's napkin nicely and put it back into its ring—until the coffee. But the coffee once drunk,

71]

down the back stairs into the pantry and the best of
luck. The law of the jungle comes into its own.
Dammit, there's no need to be a complete fool....
Quiet! I haven't finished. I can see the way your
mind's working. You are young, you want the moon—
you are going to say, "That's middle-class hypocrisy,
What about ideals? Where does the ideal come in?"

SECRETARY:

Yes, sir.

GENERAL:

Well, my boy, the ideal is doing very nicely, thank
you. The ideal, my friend, is the lifebuoy. You're in
the ocean, splashing about, doing your damndest not
to drown, in spite of whirlpools and cross currents. The
main thing is to do the regulation breast-stroke and if
you're not a clod, never to let the lifebuoy out of your
sight. No one expects any more than that of you.
If you relieve yourself in the water now and then,
that's your affair. The sea is big, and if the top half of
your body still looks as though it's doing the regulation
breaststroke, nobody will say a word.

SECRETARY:

But does one never reach the lifebuoy, General?

GENERAL:

Never. But if your heart's in the right place, you never
lose sight of it either. Fanatics who try a faster stroke
to reach it at all costs, deluge everybody else and
always finish up by drowning, generally dragging God
knows how many poor devils under with them, who
could otherwise have gone on quietly floundering

[72

about and minding their own business. Do you see what I mean?

SECRETARY:

No, sir. Might I say something, though?

GENERAL:

Go ahead, my boy. Your turn to speak now.

SECRETARY:

I am twenty years old, General. I would rather try to go fast and drown.

GENERAL:

Gently, after a pause.

You are right, my boy, It's a sorry business, growing old, and understanding.

In a sudden cry.

Lieutenant St. Pé! Graduated second from Saumur! Volunteer! Wait for me! I'm done for anyway—here goes, I'd rather drown! I only said all that because one has to. Try all the same not to drown others, even in a good cause. That's what weighs heavy on a man, hurting other people. I have got used to everything, but not to that.

GENERAL'S WIFE:

Off.

Leon!

GENERAL:

Yes!

WIFE:

Leon, where are you?

73]

GENERAL:

Wearily.

I'm here! I'm here, for Heaven's sake! I'm always here.

WIFE:

Off.

Come and sit with me, Leon. Goodness only knows what you're playing at while you think I'm asleep.

GENERAL:

Looking at the SECRETARY with a smile.

Playing the fool, my dear, with a young spark who wasn't even listening and quite right he was too, damn him!

Slapping him on the back.

Wait a bit, my boy. There's no almighty hurry after all, even if they do make fun of you. Wait until the right girl comes along and with her you will miraculously cease to be afraid. But when you find her, by Hades don't wait seventeen years!

SECRETARY:

I won't, sir.

GENERAL:

At once! Remember my advice! Immediately! And make for the lifebuoy, side by side—the only proper way to swim is two by two. Wish me luck. I'm going in myself. But it's on the cards that one of us may drown en route.

WIFE:

Leon!

He goes into her room.

[74

GENERAL:

Here I am, Madam. At your service for the last time.

SECRETARY:

At once! That's all I'll keep of his advice!
> *He takes his courage in both hands and goes into the morning room.* MLLE. DE STE-EUVERTE *is heard murmuring through the half-open door.*

MLLE. DE STE-E.:

Leon! Leon, you've come back! Can it be true then? Will I really never be alone again? Oh! Leon!
> *A* pause. *Re-enter the* SECRETARY *red as a beetroot.*

SECRETARY:

The lady is still making a mistake. And yet, despite the action of the sedative, something tells me that she isn't altogether taken in. How interesting it is, living! The Reverend Fathers never told me.
> *He screws up his courage and goes back into the room.*

Black Out

Curtain

ACT TWO

SCENE TWO

The same, except that the wall which hid the the General's Wife's room from view has been removed. It is afternoon. The shutters have been closed in the General's room, now deserted, as well as in the other. The GENERAL'S WIFE, *in night cap and bedjacket is sitting up among her pillows in her monumental quilted bed. The* GENERAL *is standing.*

GENERAL:

We must thrash this matter out, Madam, once and for all.

GENERAL'S WIFE:

I tried to kill myself, you monster, isn't that enough for you?

GENERAL:

You were stretched out on the tracks—an awkward position but quite safe. The train had already passed.

WIFE:

I didn't know! I was waiting for it!

GENERAL:

On that branch line you could reckon on a good twenty-four hours of it.

[76

WIFE:

Is nothing sacred to you? You brute! I might have died of cold during the night.

GENERAL:

We are well into April, and spring is early this year. We are dying of heat.

WIFE:

Of sunstroke then—starvation, I don't know. . . . Of sorrow—yes, that's it—quite simply of sorrow, in my state of health.

GENERAL:

Sorrow you can die of in your bed, Madam, at leisure. It was absurd, like everything else you do.

WIFE:

I am seriously ill. How often has the doctor told you that my condition gives cause for the gravest alarm? I did truly mean to kill myself and that alone should make you fall sobbing at my feet, if your heart were not made of granite!

GENERAL:

My heart is not made of granite, Madam, but I am thrifty with my tears.

WIFE:

I sacrificed my life for you!
        Screaming.
Murderer!

GENERAL:

Be quiet, confound you, or I'll leave the room! Let us talk things over calmly.

77]

WIFE:

I'm too unhappy. You aren't unhappy, not you! You
have your health and strength, you have. You're up
and dressed each morning, you ride your horse, you
walk around the garden, you go drinking with your
friends! You live! You jeer at me, on your two legs,
while I sit glued to my wheelchair. Aren't you ashamed
of being well?

GENERAL:

You are glued to your wheelchair for no other reason
than because you want to be. We know that now.

WIFE:

Do you dare to say that I'm not ill?

GENERAL:

One has to be an idiot like myself, Madam, to go on
believing in your aches and pains by this time. As for
your poor ailing legs, thank God we'll hear no more
about those for a bit. I strongly suspect you of stretch-
ing them in your room every night. They helped you
keep your balance mighty well down the wisteria and
over to the railway line this morning.

WIFE:

It was the last spasm of the stricken beast who longs
for death— Call your accomplice Doctor Bonfant, with
his rubber mallet; let him test my reflexes!

GENERAL:

Death and damnation, Madam, that's too easy!

[78

WIFE:

Too easy for you, I daresay. What have you got to complain about? While I lie here, racked with pain, you who can wander fancy free on your great fat legs, where do you go, eh?

GENERAL:

From my study to the garden, at your beck and call every ten minutes.

WIFE:

And what is there in the garden? Answer me that, you pig, you satyr, you lascivious goat!

GENERAL:

Well, I dunno . . . roses. . . .

WIFE:

Cackling.

Roses! There's Madame Tardieu on the other side of the privet hedge, that frightful woman who exhibits her bodice as she leans over her flowerbeds. They're a household word hereabouts, Madame Tardieu's breasts! Whalebone, rubber, steel probably—she's propped up like a tumbledown barn.

GENERAL:

All right, all right, all right! After all, I haven't been to look.

WIFE:

You dream of nothing else. You'll be mighty disillusioned when the great day comes! But on the other side of the fence, at the bottom of the garden, walking along the school path at midday and at four, there are

younger ones, aren't there? The little convent girls!
You centaur! One of these days the parents will complain.

GENERAL:

You're wandering, Madam. They say good morning to
me, and I say good morning back.

WIFE:

And what about prize-giving day, at which you always
manage to officiate, you old faun! When you kiss
them, red as a lobster in your uniform?

GENERAL:

It's the custom.

WIFE:

What you're thinking isn't the custom and you know
it! You tickle their bosoms with your decorations as
you lean over them. Don't say you don't. I've seen you.

GENERAL:

If nothing worse happens to them as they're growing
up we'll make May Queens out of them!

WIFE:

Queens of the May, indeed! You're always ready to
officiate on May Day too. Last year's one, that hussy,
as you kissed her, you whispered something in her ear.
It was reported to me.

GENERAL:

> *Chaffingly.*

I whispered something? You don't say so?

[80

WIFE:

You arranged to meet her, I know. Besides I've seen her since. She's pregnant.

GENERAL:

Nonsense, she's put on weight, that's all.

WIFE:

My maids are putting on weight too, one after the other.

GENERAL:

Let's change the subject, Madam. I have something very serious to say to you. You are untrue to me, Madam, that's the long and the short of it. You wrote to Doctor Bonfant that you were in love with him. I have proof of it here in my wallet, down in black and white with two spelling mistakes which identify your hand. Yes. For you, who have always accused me of being a clodhopper, too lumpish to appreciate Baudelaire or Wagner, can't tell a conjunction from a carrot. You never had a day's schooling in your life.

WIFE:

How shabby you are! To come on my deathbed and throw my unhappy childhood in my face! For over a year I was a boarder with the daughters of consuls and ambassadors in the most select ladies' college in Paris.

GENERAL:

Where your mother went to do the household mending and where they took you in and fed you out of charity.

81]

WIFE:

My poor mother and I suffered a great deal, no doubt.
But please to remember that my mother was a woman
of infinite distinction, not a little provincial housewife
like yours.

GENERAL:

One trade is as good as another, but your mother,
Madam, was a dresser at the Opera.

WIFE:

She accepted the post at the earnest request of the
Director, solely for love of music. A woman whose
hand M. Gounod kissed at a gala matinee for charity.

GENERAL:

Have it your own way. Let us get back to those letters.
Did you or did you not write them? Do you or do you
not address him as "Armand"? Do you tell him, yes
or no, that his hair smells of vanilla when he sounds
your chest, and that you pretend to have a belly ache so
he can come and feel it for you? It's down in black
and white with two spelling mistakes in your own handwriting.

WIFE:

How could you stoop so low as to come poking about
in my correspondence?

GENERAL:

I did not poke about in your correspondence, Madam.
I obtained possession of those letters. How? That's
none of your business.

[82

WIFE:

Oh, isn't it? None of my business? Those letters were in the drawer of my bedside table where I keep my curlers and other objects of an intimate nature. You tell me they are in your wallet. And you dare to cross-question *me*? It's past belief! But I did think you were still a gentleman.

GENERAL:

Dammit, Madam, will you stick to the point?

WIFE:

So you ransack a lady's drawers, do you, my lad? You try to dishonor her, you a senior officer? All right, then, I shall tell. I shall tell everybody. I shall get up, I'll recover, for a day, the use of my poor aching legs, and the night of the reception at the annual Tattoo, in front of all the high ranking military personnel, I shall make a sensational entrance and I shall tell all!

GENERAL:

I repeat I have not ransacked your drawers.

WIFE:

Have you those letters?

GENERAL:

I have.

WIFE:

Show them to me.

GENERAL:

Ha ha! Not on your life.

WIFE:

Very well. If you really have those letters in your
wallet, there can be nothing more between us but an
ocean of contempt. You may go. I am sleepy. I'm
asleep.
> *She lies with her eyes closed.*

GENERAL:

No, Madam, you are not asleep. That would be too
easy. Open your eyes. Open your eyes, this instant, do
you hear, or I'll open them for you!
> *Shaking her.*

Emily! Do as I say! Open your eyes!
> *He shakes her, slaps her, forces her eyelids up
> from their white eyeballs, begins to lose his
> head.*

Come to your senses, damn you! What new game are
you playing now?

WIFE:
> *Weakly.*

My heart!

GENERAL:

What about your heart!

WIFE:

It's shrinking. Goodbye, Leon! I never loved anyone
else but you.

GENERAL:

Oh no, not your heart attack. We haven't even raised
our voices. Your heart attack is for after the big scenes,

[84

Madam. You are warm, your pulse is good. I'm not falling for that.

Shaking her.

Wake up, Emily! You can't be as rigid as that. You're doing it on purpose. I'll give you your drops.

He rummages about among the bottles on the side table.

Holy Moses, what a collection! It would take a qualified druggist to make head or tail of this lot! There's enough here to upset the constitution of a cart horse. Needless to say, no dropper. Where the devil did Eugenie put the thing? Oh well, here goes—one drop more, one drop less—the way things are now. . . . There, Emily, drink this, and if that doesn't do the trick I'll call the doctor. Unclench your teeth, my love—unclench your teeth, damn you, it's dripping all over you! Give me strength—what's the matter with you? Your pulse is all right. There's no getting away from that. I'll give you your injection.

WIFE:

Feebly.

You're still rummaging, Leon. You're suspicious of me even on my deathbed.

GENERAL:

I'm *not* rummaging, I'm looking for your capsules.

WIFE:

Too late. Call the children.

GENERAL:

What are you raving about, my dear, you aren't going to die. You're weak, that's all. I'll get the doctor.

85]

WIFE:

Too late. I implore you, don't move, Leon. Stay with me. Hold my hand as you did in the old days long ago, when I was ill. You took care of me then, you were patient with me. You used to bathe my temples with eau de cologne and murmur sweet nothings in my ears. . . .

GENERAL:

Looking for the bottle and mumbling.
I can still dab you with a bit of cologne. . . .

WIFE:

But without the sweet nothings! It's that that's killing me—you murderer!

GENERAL:

He bathes her face.
There. That will revive you.

WIFE:

It frightens you, eh, to hear me say it? I'm dying for want of your love, Leon!

GENERAL:

No, no, no, don't be silly now. To begin with you are not dying at all, and you know perfectly well, my love, that I am always full of attentions for you.

WIFE:

Attentions! What do I want with attentions! I want you to love me as you used to long ago, Leon, when you took me in your arms and called me your little girl, when you bit me all over. Aren't I your little girl any more, to be carried naked to my bath?

[86

GENERAL:

Uncomfortably.

Emily, we all have to grow up sometime.

WIFE:

Plaintively.

Why don't you bite me all over like a young terrier any more?

GENERAL:

More and more embarrassed.

Dammit, Madam, young terriers grow into old ones, after twenty years. Besides, I've lost my teeth.

WIFE:

Sitting up with astonishing vigor considering her heart attack.

You've teeth enough for others, you mealy-mouthed old fraud! You can talk about those letters which were never even sent. I have evidence of another sort, in a trinket box underneath my mattress, letters both sent and received, where there's no question of your having lost your teeth. Letters in which you play the young man for another's benefit—and there you flatter yourself incidentally, my poor Leon—for apart from your summary prowess with the maids, you needn't think you're capable of much in that line either——

GENERAL:

Be quiet, Madam! What do you know about it?

WIFE:

I know as much as all women left unsatisfied. Learn first to satisfy one woman, to be a man in her bed, before you go scampering into the beds of others.

87]

GENERAL:

So I have never been a man in your bed, Madam. Is that it?

WIFE:

Soon weary, my friend, soon asleep, and when for a wonder you had a little energy, soon replete. We would both close our eyes in the bed, but while you performed your little task, picturing the Lord knows whom, you don't imagine, do you, that it was you I thought about?

GENERAL:

How vulgar you are, Madam—vulgar and shameless. However, if that was so, why the reproaches and the scenes, why so many tears for so long?

WIFE:

Because you belong to me, Leon! You are mine like my house, mine like my jewels, mine like my furniture, mine like your name.

GENERAL:

And is that what you understand by love?

WIFE:

> *In a great and frightful cry, standing on her bed in her nightshirt, a nightmarish figure.*

Yes!

GENERAL:

Death and damnation, Madam! I do not belong to you!

WIFE:

To whom then?

[88

GENERAL:

To no one. To myself perhaps.

WIFE:

No! Not any longer. I am your wife. Your wife before
God and before the law.

GENERAL:

Hell's bells, Madam, I'll escape you!

WIFE:

Never!

GENERAL:

I'll pretend not to know you.

WIFE:

I'll scream, I'll cause a riot! I'll break things, I'll run
up debts to ruin you—

GENERAL:

I tell you I'll take a train and disappear into thin air.
You won't know where I am.

WIFE:

You'd never dare, and if you did, I'd follow you to the
far ends of the earth!

GENERAL:

And when I die, hell's teeth! Will you make that
journey too?

WIFE:

When you die I shall cry out loud—I was his wife! I
shall put on widow's weeds, I, and I alone, will have
the right and I shall visit your grave on All Souls' Day.
I'll have my name engraved on the tombstone and

when my turn comes to die I shall come and lie beside
you for eternity. Unknown people, as they pass, will
still read that I was your wife, on the stone!

GENERAL:
By God I hate you, Madam.

WIFE:
What difference does that make? I am your wife.

GENERAL:
I hate the sight and sound of you! And I'll tell you
something else that's stronger even than my hatred
and disgust. I am dying of boredom, Madam, by your
side.

WIFE:
You bore me too, but I am your wife just the same
and about that you can do nothing.

GENERAL:
But devil take you, you hate me just as much!

WIFE:
Yes, I hate you. You ruined my career. I had a superb
voice, a dazzling future—you insisted that I give up
the stage. All that was brilliant in me you crushed
underfoot. Other men worshipped me, you frightened
them away with your great sword. You created a desert
around me with your stupid jealousy, you made me
unlearn how to be beautiful—unlearn how to love and
be loved. Expected me to keep house for you like a
servant, feed your sickly children, I, whose breasts were
famous throughout Paris!

[90

GENERAL:

Your breasts famous? Don't make me laugh. Where did you exhibit them anyway, in Lohengrin?

WIFE:

At festivals of Art. Before people whose refinement and luxurious living your petty tradesman's world can't even guess at. Have you ever thought, you desperado, of all I sacrificed for you?

GENERAL:

Death and damnation, that is ancient history, Madam! I am resolved to sue for a divorce.

WIFE:

A divorce! You could never live alone, you're far too frightened. Who do you think would have you, you poor devil?

GENERAL:

I have found someone who will have me.

WIFE:

She must be very old and pretty ugly—or pretty poor to be reduced to that.

GENERAL:

It's a lie. She is young and beautiful. She's true to me. She is waiting for me.

WIFE:

Since when?

GENERAL:

Since seventeen years.

WIFE:

You must be joking, my dear! Seventeen years! And you think she loves you? And you, do you think you love her? And they've been waiting seventeen years, poor lambs!

GENERAL:

Yes, Madam, and because of you.

WIFE:

Oh, Leon, if I weren't so ill, I'd laugh; I'd laugh like a mad one! It's too silly—really too silly! Seventeen years! But if you really loved her, you poor imbecile, you would have left me long ago!

GENERAL:

I stayed out of respect for your grief and pity for your illness, which I long took to be genuine, Madam.

WIFE:

What a fool you are! Do you think I couldn't dance if I wanted to?
She gets out of bed.
Look! You see how well I can stand! Come and dance with me. Come!
She sings and dances a few steps.

GENERAL:

Let me go! You're mad. Go back to bed.

WIFE:

No. You are my true love and I want to dance with you. Like at the Ball at the Military College in Saumur, the one of '93, seventeen years ago, funnily enough. Do you remember?

[92

GENERAL:

Confound you, why?

WIFE:

Because you were so handsome and scintillating and sure of yourself with the women at that Ball. "Major St. Pé!" How smartly you clicked your heels, German fashion, when you introduced yourself! How fetchingly you smoothed your whiskers, how prettily you kissed their hands! I shall never forget that ball. I was still in love with you then, and I had stayed faithful, idiot that I was, in spite of your lady friends whom you forced me to invite to dinner. But at that ball I suddenly had enough, all at once, in a space of a second. You were dancing a waltz with a fair ninny of a girl—I saw you whisper in her ear and she made eyes at you and simpered. The Waltz of the Toreadors. . . . I even remember the tune.

>   *She sings.*

I. was too wretched. I had to get away, out of that ballroom. I went out into the hall to order my carriage. There was a man there, younger and handsomer than you, and he helped me. And when he found our carriage he said I couldn't possibly go home alone and he climbed in to escort me.

GENERAL:

Well?

WIFE:

Well, you were still waltzing, my poor dear, with your superb half turns and your airs and graces. What do you suppose women are made of? He became my lover.

93]

GENERAL:

What? You have had a lover, Madam, and it was at
that Saumur Ball that you made his acquaintance? A
man who had merely helped you find our carriage, a
complete stranger?—I won't even ask you his rank.
How horrible! But I'd like to believe that you had a
few doubts, dear God, a few misgivings, before taking
such a step. I fondly hope you did at least wait a little?

WIFE:

Of course, my dear. I was a respectable woman. I
waited.

GENERAL:

How long?

WIFE:

Three days.

GENERAL:

Exploding.

Holy suffering rattlesnakes, I waited seventeen years,
Madam, and I'm waiting still!

WIFE:

And when that one was posted, I forget where, to the
devil—to the Far East, I took another just as handsome, and another, and again another, and so on before I grew too old and there would only be you left
who would have me.

GENERAL:

But dammit, if you were untrue to me why the tears
and the reproaches—why the immense heartaches and
the torment—why this illness?

[94

WIFE:

To keep you, Leon. To keep you for always because
I am your wife. For I do love you, Leon, on top of
everything. I hate you for all the harm you did to
me, but I love you—not tenderly, you fool, not with
seventeen years of waiting and letter-writing—not for
the bliss of being in your arms at night—we have never
made love together, you poor wretch and you know
it—not for your conversation—you bore me—not for
your rank either, nor your money—I've been offered
more—I love you because you are mine, my object, my
thing, my hold-all, my garbage bin——

GENERAL:

No!

WIFE:

Yes, and you know it! And whatever you may promise
others you know you will never be anything but that.

GENERAL:

Wildly.

No!

WIFE:

Yes! You will never be able to bring yourself to hurt
me, you're too cowardly. You know it, and you know
I know it, too.

GENERAL:

No!

WIFE:

Yes! Come now, darling, dance with me. The Waltz
of the Toreadors, the last waltz, with me this time.

GENERAL:

No!

WIFE:

Yes! I want you to. And you want whatever I want. Come, dance with your chronic invalid, your old bag of bones. Come dance with your remorse! Come, dance with your love!

GENERAL:

Don't touch me, for pity's sake, don't touch me!

> *She pursues him. He cringes in a corner. All of a sudden he stretches out his arms, grips her throat and yells.*

Phantasmagoria!!

> *The GENERAL'S WIFE struggles in her voluminous nightgown, trying to tear his hands away from her throat.*

Black Out

ACT THREE

ACT THREE

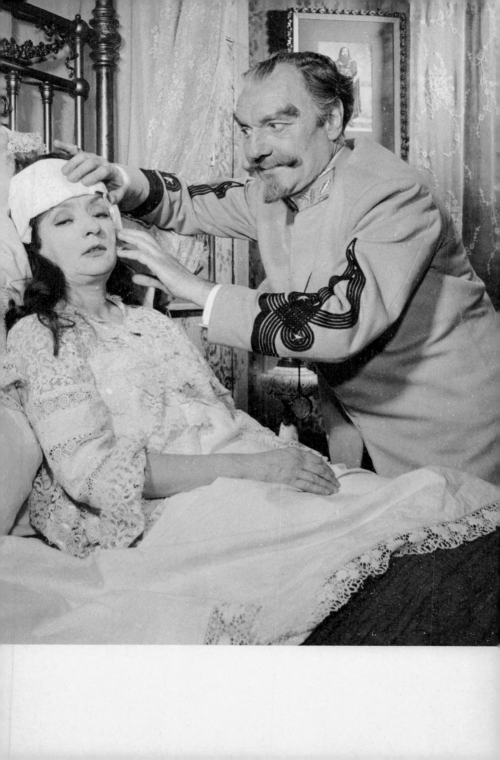

ACT THREE

When the lights go up, the wall of the General's Wife's room is back in place. The GENERAL *is alone in his study. It is evening. He prowls about like a caged bear, a shadow in the gathering darkness. All of a sudden he stops and cries out. Bugle is heard. He takes binoculars and peers out window as the* DOCTOR *comes out of Mme. St. Pé's room. The* GENERAL *looks at him in silence.*

DOCTOR:
I have just taken her blood pressure. She's as right as rain. She's had a bad fright, that's all.

GENERAL:
So did I.

DOCTOR:
So did I, my friend. The moment your maid appeared and said to come at once, I guessed Madame was choking.

GENERAL:
What did she say?

99]

DOCTOR:

Who? Your maid?

GENERAL:

My wife.

DOCTOR:

My poor friend, she seems to think it quite in order that you should want to do away with her. Murder is the regular concomitant of passion at the opera. She submits gracefully, biding her time, no doubt, and feeling vaguely flattered: she is more than ever convinced that you are a pair of sublime and star-crossed lovers.

GENERAL:

Oh, the idiocy of it! Will she never understand that she quite simply bores me?

DOCTOR:

I'm afraid you will have to face up to it, General. Never.

GENERAL:

But, dear God, that can't be all there is to life! Why did no one ever warn me? Everybody looks happy round about me, and content. How do they do it, damn them—how do they manage not to suffer? What is their password? Let them tell it me, at once. I've no more time to wait.

DOCTOR:

My dear old friend, I think that is a question one must ask oneself when one is very much younger.

GENERAL:
> *Yelling.*

I *am* young! Lieutenant St. Pé! I decline all other rank! It's nothing but a booby-trap! I see it now.
> *Suddenly.*

Doctor, has medicine not discovered anything to put the clock back seventeen years?

DOCTOR:
Nothing so far.

GENERAL:
Are you sure?

DOCTOR:
It would surely have been mentioned in certain . . . specialist publications.

GENERAL:
Are you aware of what's going on? Mlle. de Ste-Euverte and my secretary have gone out for a walk. They've been away nearly two hours.

DOCTOR:
Nothing very odd about that. You were closeted with your wife. Your explanations bode fair to going on forever. I expect they simply decided to go for a short stroll while they were waiting.

GENERAL:
A curious misunderstanding arose between the two of them this morning. Then they left, with their little fingers linked, so the maid tells me. Does that strike you as normal too? As for my daughters, who were enamoured of our hero—they have gone as well, leav-

ing this letter on the table, together with their fake jewellery wrapped up in tissue paper.

He pulls a letter out of his pocket.

"We are too unhappy. He is in love with another. We prefer to die"—(two more of them, it's all the rage in this house)—"Tell Mme. Dupont-Fredaine not to go on with our dresses." Among other primordial virtues their mother has imbued them with a solid notion of economy.

DOCTOR:

Good Heavens, and haven't they come home yet?

GENERAL:

I sent the gardener in search of them. They must be down by the pond, dabbling their feet in the water. They're far too plain to kill themselves. Everything is tumbling about my ears! Dear God, how will it all end?

DOCTOR:

As in real life—or in the theatre, in the days when plays *were* plays—a contrived dénouement, not too gloomy on the face of it, and which doesn't really fool a soul, and then a little later—curtain. I speak for myself as well as you. Your blood pressure's up to two hundred and fifty and my gall bladder is a bag of stones. Make way for the young! May they commit the self-same follies and die of the same diseases.

GENERAL:

But I love her, Doctor, and I am young!

Enter the MAID. *Lights lamp on R. table.*

[102

MAID:

Will you please say if I am to serve dinner, sir? If we wait much longer, the deviled mushrooms won't be deviled mushrooms any more.

GENERAL:

Oh shut up about your mushrooms! We'll call them something else, then.

MAID:

And there's Father Ambrose drinking white wine in the pantry. He says he'll wait as long as you please, sir, but what he has to tell you is too important to put off till tomorrow.

GENERAL:

Feed him the deviled mushrooms. What does he want, today of all days?

MAID:

I already suggested he should eat something. He won't. He says the excitement of what he has to tell you has quite spoilt his appetite. But, my word, he's catching up on the white wine! I don't know if he helps himself like that at Mass but if you don't see him soon, whatever it is he has to tell you is going to be pretty muddled. I think he's going off his head. He can't wait to say some Masses in thanksgiving. He says it's Providence.

GENERAL:

Why, what's Providence been up to this time?

MAID:
He says he can tell no one but yourself, sir. It's a secret between Providence and him.

GENERAL:
Well, tell them both to wait.
Exit MAID.
My reason is tottering, I can feel it. I can't have lost her so stupidly after seventeen years the way one loses a dog in the street. With her lost to me, there's nothing left but a ludicrous old pantaloon, who never saw a single one of his gestures through to its conclusion. I have the impression that Lieutenant St. Pé is lying bloodless on a field of battle, not even wounded in the fight—some idiot's rifle blew up in his back a few minutes before zero hour—but that all the same he is going to die. Doctor, if I've lost her——

DOCTOR:
Who has been looking out of the window.
No, General, you have not lost her. Here she is, with her ravisher.
The SECRETARY, *tomato-red, and* GHISLAINE, *her eyes on the ground, appear in the door-way.*

GENERAL:
Rushing forward in relief.
Ghislaine . . . this unaccountable stroll—I nearly died of fright. Now will you kindly tell me. . . .

GHIS.:

In her usual slightly solemn manner.
My dear, will you ask the doctor to leave us for a
moment? Gaston, leave us too, please.

SECRETARY:

Self-assured though a little somber.
Very well. But only for a moment.

GENERAL:

Only for a moment? What's got into the young
puppy? He never dared speak in that tone to anyone in
his life before!

DOCTOR:

To the GENERAL *on his way out.*
Courage, Lieutenant! Something tells me this is going
to be your last campaign.
        GASTON *and the* DOCTOR *go out.*

GENERAL:

Timidly.
Are you going to explain, Ghislaine?

GHIS.:

Yes, my dear, I'll tell you. It's quite simple. I love
that young man.

GENERAL:

You're joking. And it isn't funny, Ghislaine. Why,
thundering Hades, two hours ago you'd never even
seen the fellow!

GHIS.:

Had I seen you before the Saumur Ball? And yet the
very second when you took me by the waist I fell in

105]

love with you. Those seventeen years took nothing away, but added nothing, either, to my love.

GENERAL:
That wonderful mad gift of yourself in one moment is something I have always understood and loved you for. But this isn't the same thing at all.

GHIS.:
Why isn't it, Leon?

GENERAL:
Well, because . . . at the Saumur Ball—it was me.

GHIS:
            Gently.
Well?

GENERAL:
Well, dammit all, it's not for me to say so, but I was brilliant, I was witty, I was young! And I desired you madly—that counts for something too. But him!

GHIS:
He is retiring—or he was—a little naïve, perhaps, but you see, my dear—now how can I put it? For a woman those are opposing qualities, but equally appealing— we love everything. It's like having to choose at a fitting, between a green silk and a pink one. I might add that he is young, younger even than you were at Saumur, and that he desires me too.

GENERAL:
            Spluttering with laughter.
Him? That nonentity? That mooncalf?

[106

GHIS:

Leon, I forbid you to insult him!

GENERAL:

Beside himself.

Try and stop me! So he desires you, does he? Do you
expect me to believe that when he saw you his anaemic
blood gave one leap? Don't make me laugh. Say he was
speechless—say he knelt at your feet, recited poetry
perhaps—but don't tell me the boy desires you—it's
grotesque!

GHIS.:

But he proved it, my dear.

GENERAL:

How? How could he have proved it to you?

Trying one last hope.

Let a real man, worthy of that title, take you in his
arms tonight—and it will be tonight, my dearest, I
swear it—let a real man once make love to you, God
dammit; and all the rest will disappear like so much
smoke.

GHIS.:

Superbly.

I know. It *is* all so much smoke, my dear. Because at
long last, someone has made love to me. I'll shout it
to the world, I'm not ashamed. What words do you
need then to make you understand? I belong to him.

GENERAL:

He dared? That two-faced, vice-ridden little villain? ! !
That brute? Took you by force, did he? I'll kill him!

GHIS.:

No, no, my dear, not by force. He took me, and I gave myself, and I am his now, for always.

GENERAL:

Stricken, holds out his hands to her, suddenly humble.

Ghislaine, it's all a nightmare. I'll help you to forget it. . . .

GHIS.:

Drawing away from him.

No, Leon, you must not touch me any more. Only he may touch me now. And you should know how faithful I can be.

GENERAL:

But when he touched you, you had fallen on your head, you were pumped full of sedative, you didn't even know who was touching you. You thought it was me!

GHIS.:

The first few times, yes. But afterwards I knew quite well. He touched me, really touched me! And all of a sudden I was no longer sad and lonely and drifting with the tide, I found my footing on the shore at last and I shall never be alone again—at tables, at Mass, in my wide, wide bed. Don't you see what a wonderful adventure it is? You would be a tiny bit glad, too, if you really loved me, Leon.

GENERAL:

I do love you, Ghislaine, but——

GHIS.:

Then why not share my joy and let everyone be happy?
Crying out.
I am not alone any more! You so often wished it for
me. You used to say I should have a companion——

GENERAL:

Yes, but a female——

GHIS.:

I have a male companion now, it's so much better!
We'll meet from time to time just as we used to do.
He said he would permit it. Although, between ourselves, my dear, I rather doubt it. He's insanely jealous,
do you know that? He says he won't let me out of his
sight! Oh, my dear, I am so happy. I am no longer
a dog without a collar. I have a little cord around my
neck with my owner's name on it. How good it feels.

GENERAL:

Lieutenant St. Pé! Don't leave me! What is happening?

GHIS.:

Heedless of the interruption.
You say he has no wit. Not with men, perhaps, not
with you, but what does that matter to me? To me
he says the prettiest things. He told me that we must
swim abreast towards the ideal as if towards a lifebuoy, and that the only proper way to swim is two by
two.

109]

GENERAL:

I might have known it! Did he also tell you that life was one long family lunch, with napkin rings, forks of different shapes and sizes and a bell push under the table?

GHIS.:

What are you suggesting, spiteful? He says poetic things. He says life is but a holiday, a ball. . . .

GENERAL:

With an involuntary cry of pain.
A ball . . .

GHIS.:

Yes, isn't that a sweet idea? A ball of a night, and we must make haste he says, before the lamps go out. I loved him from the very first, I told you so, but I had got so into the way of thinking love was nothing but one endless vigil, that when he asked me to be his I wanted to cry—Later! Tomorrow! Do you know what he said?

GENERAL:

In a strangled voice.
No!

GHIS.:

Triumphantly.
He said, "At once! At once, my darling!" Now who but he would say a thing like that? At once! It's wonderful. I never guessed that one could have something at once!
The SECRETARY enters, his suspicions aroused but resolved to stand no nonsense.

[110

SECRETARY:

The moment is up, Ghislaine.

GHIS.:

Flustered.

I'm sorry, Gaston.

GENERAL:

Bearing down on him.

I'm sorry, Gaston! So there you are, Don Juan! The pretty turtle doves. Just look at them, will you? It's enough to make a cat laugh. What the devil do you take me for, the pair of you? Death and damnation, I'll soon show you what I'm made of!

The DOCTOR appears in the doorway.

Come in, Doctor, come in. You're just in time. Do you know what they've just told me, these two starry-eyed cherubs here? They're in love with each other, if you please. Yes, sir, since two hours ago! And what's more, they haven't wasted any time. Some folks have a scruple or two, some folks wait a little while—not they! In the woods, anyhow, like animals. And they expect my blessing into the bargain! God almighty, have they completely lost every scrap of moral sense?

DOCTOR:

Gently.

Lieutenant St. Pé.

GENERAL:

Thundering.

General! Please to address me by my proper rank! I'll show them who I am! I am going to put on my uniform and all my decorations. No, it'll take too long. Aha, so you seduce young girls, do you, eh? Steal another man's wife, would you? Play cock of the roost, sir, would you? Well, me young jacko, when you've got guts you must show 'em, and otherwise than with the ladies—and that may not prove quite so funny. Fetch me two swords, someone! Those two up there, on the wall.

He climbs onto a chair to unhook them.

And no need for seconds either. The Doctor can stand by.

GHIS.:

Oh, my God, he wants blood! He's a cannibal!

DOCTOR:

General, you aren't going to start all that again?

GENERAL:

And you down there, you hold your tongue, too, sir! I haven't forgotten that business of the letters.

GHIS.:

Holding his legs.

Leon! I love him! And if you love me, as you say, you won't hurt him.

GENERAL:

The hell I will! I'll cut his ears off, Madam! I'll kill him!

DOCTOR:

General, get down off that chair!

[112

SECRETARY:
>*With great nobility.*
Though I have never held a sword, if the General insists, I am prepared to fight.

GHIS.:
Gaston, not you! Not you! Let him fight by himself!

DOCTOR:
General, it would be murder! He's a child!

GENERAL:
>*Still struggling to get the swords down.*
There are no children any more. If he's a child let him go and play with his hoop. Holy suffering blood-stained billicans, who's the double-dyed blockhead who put up these swords! ! !
>*Calling unthinkingly.*
Gaston!

SECRETARY:
>*Running up.*
Yes, sir?

GENERAL:
Give me a hand, my boy.

SECRETARY:
>*Keen.*
Yes, sir.
>*He climbs on to a chair.*

113]

GENERAL:

What the devil are you doing there, sir? Get down! Doctor, come and help me will you?

DOCTOR:

General, I refuse to be a party any longer to this tragic tomfoolery. You have no right to provoke this lad.

GENERAL:

Did he or did he not consider himself old enough to take the woman I love?

GHIS.:

But you never would take her at all!

GENERAL:

I know my manners. Besides, I was going to.
        He changes his mind and turns on his chair.
Why, what a fool I am! It's so much simpler than that! Come to think of it, he *is* a child.
        Paternally.
How old are you exactly, my boy?

SECRETARY:

Twenty in strawberry-time, sir. The twenty-third of May.

GENERAL:

Twenty in strawberry-time, splendid. In order to marry then, unless I'm much mistaken, you need your parents' consent, do you not?

[114

SECRETARY:

Why recall in her presence the painful circumstances attendant on my birth? I have no parents, sir, as you well know. I am a foundling.

GENERAL:

Climbing down from the chair.

True. But you have a guardian, have you not, a venerable churchman, Father Lambert I think I'm right in saying? We'll see if Father Lambert will consent to the marriage when I've told him a thing or two!

The GENERAL *goes to the door and shouts down the stairs.*

Eugenie! Eugenie! The Curé! The Curé, quickly! Send Father Ambrose up at the double! She's quite right, it *is* Providence that brings the fellow here, for once. I'll bet my braces Father Lambert will never let you marry an adventuress!

GHIS.:

Oh, Leon! How could you?

Enter the PRIEST.

GENERAL:

Ah, there you are, Father.

FATHER AMBROSE:

General, at last!

GENERAL:

You take the words out of my mouth.

GENERAL ⎱ A matter of the utmost importance ...

FATHER A. ⎰ A revelation of the utmost interest ...

115]

GENERAL ⎤ The peace and honor of the family. A watch-
⎟ ful firmness ...
⎟
FATHER A. ⎢ The joy and sanctification of the home.
⎦ A sacred duty. ...

GENERAL:

After you.

FATHER A.:

After you. No, on the second thoughts, me first. General, may I speak freely before everyone?

GENERAL:

If you like. But make haste. I'm in a hurry.

FATHER A.:

But we are all friends here, I see—friends who will
soon be as deeply moved as I. ...

SECRETARY:

If I am in the way, General, I can withdraw.

FATHER A.:

   Mysteriously.

No, my son, you are not in the way. Far from it. General, it is with deep emotion that I recognize in this
the hand of Providence. ...

GENERAL:

No preambles! Come to the point, Father, come to the
point. I have to talk to you about this young rascal
here.

FATHER A.:

So have I. When I brought Gaston to you for the post
of secretary, I had indeed no inkling. ...

GENERAL:

Come to the point, I say. I'm an old soldier. In a couple of words.

FATHER A.:

Heaven has nevertheless willed it, in its infinite mansuetude and the exquisite delicacy of its Grace. . . .

GENERAL:

In a couple of words! Not a syllable more or else I'll speak myself.

FATHER A.:

Very well. You have asked for it, General, but it may sound a little crude. Montauban. Lea.

GENERAL:

What do you mean, Montauban Lea. What's that, an address?

FATHER A.:

You see how difficult it is in a couple of words. Allow me to amplify a little. There lived in 1890 at Montauban, where the 8th Dragoons were on maneuvers, a young dressmaker by the name of Lea.

GENERAL:

Racking his brains.

Lea? Lea? Holy codfish, Lea! Well, what about her? You don't know what army life can be, your reverence. I could recite you a whole almanac on those lines.

FATHER A.:

There was also a dashing captain, dashing, but alas, very fickle, very careless of a young girl's honor. This captain, the whole while the maneuvers lasted, gave young Lea to believe he loved her. Perhaps indeed he did.

GENERAL:

My dear fellow, why of course! Lea! A ravishing girl, Doctor. A dark-haired filly with eyes a man could drown in—reserved, prudish almost, but in bed of an evening—oh, my dear fellow. . . !
He has inadvertently taken the CURÉ's *arm.* I beg your pardon, Father. Have you had news of this young girl, Father?

FATHER A.:

To begin with she was not exactly a young girl, General, by this time; and she has just yielded up the ghost after a very honorable marriage, releasing by her death Father Lambert of a secret.

GENERAL:

Fancy. Twenty years ago already.

FATHER A.:

Twenty years. The exact age of this young man here, less nine months.

GENERAL:

What? ! !

FATHER A.:

A child was born, unbeknownst to you, of this guilty and transient union. A child entrusted to Father Lambert who in turn entrusted him to me. Gaston, kiss your father!

[118

GENERAL:
Well, I'll be. . . .

SECRETARY:
Sobbing with emotion, throws himself into his FATHER's *arms.*
Father! My dear old Father!

GENERAL:
Don't choke me, you great oaf! Just because he tells you I'm your father there's no call to. . . . And look at the size of him!

DOCTOR:
One thinks to sow a wild oat, General, and see, what should spring up but an oak tree.

GHIS.:
In rapture.
Why then everything is quite simple, now! You are the man I have loved all along! It's you, Leon, you! Young and free, and even handsomer than your own self! I knew those hands reminded me of something——

GENERAL:
Don't overdo it, it's becoming indecent.

GHIS.:
Flying into GASTON's *arms.*
Gaston, we are free to love each other.

SECRETARY:
Thank you, father!

GENERAL:

> *Mimicking him.*

That's right! Everything is settled. Simple as pie, isn't it? Thank you, father! Ha, so I'm your father, am I? Right. I refuse to give my consent.

GHIS.:

What?

GENERAL:

Do not protest, Madam. I don't wish my son to form an alliance with just anybody. I shall make the necessary enquiries.

GHIS.:

Leon! After all this time that you've known—

SECRETARY:

Father! Dearest father! It's so good to have a father.

FATHER A.:

General! When Providence itself went to such trouble.

DOCTOR:

> *The last.*

Lieutenant St. Pé.

GENERAL:

All right. My part in this is growing more and more ridiculous. I give up. Death and damnation, let them marry, then, and never let me hear any more about anything!

> *Enter the two* GIRLS, *filthy dirty, wrapped in blankets and crying.*

Oh Lord, what is it now?

[120

ESTELLE:

We really did jump in the lake, Papa, and we swam right out to the middle——

SIDONIA:

Until we could swim no longer——

GENERAL:

Then what?

ESTELLE:

Then we came back.

GENERAL:

Quite right. You can always die some other time. He's your brother, little sillies. So you see there wasn't any need to go and drown yourselves.

THE GIRLS:

Our brother?

GENERAL:

Yes. I have just heard the news.

SECRETARY:

Embarrassed.
That simplifies everything, young ladies. Now I can love you both.

GHIS.:

Jealous.
Gaston, I forbid you!
In seventh heaven, to the others.
What a man! Isn't he dreadful?

SIDONIA:

Our brother? But, Papa, how can that be?

ESTELLE:
Why didn't Mother know?

GENERAL:
I haven't time to explain. Ask Father Ambrose. He did the trick with the help of Providence. He'll explain it all to you one day in Sunday School. They're going to be married.

ESTELLE:
Papa, if this lady is to be married, won't we need new dresses for the wedding?

GENERAL:
Acidly.
Naturally.

ESTELLE:
I want to be in duck egg blue.

SIDONIA:
And I want to be in yellow.

GENERAL:
As you please, you look ravishing in anything. Run along to Mme. Dupont-Fredaine and tell her to call in and see me about terms!

FATHER A.:
One moment, my children. I feel that Providence has more than shown today that its bounty extends over us all. The chapel is close by. What do you say to a little prayer, all together, by way of thanksgiving? Won't you join us, General? Once won't make a habit of it. Besides, I'm sure that deep down you believe in Providence.

GENERAL:

I shall have to now that it's beginning to take notice of me. But as to saying thank you, really today my heart wouldn't be in it. Tomorrow, Father, tomorrow.

GHIS.:

They all leave with the PRIEST *save the* DOCTOR *and the* GENERAL.

GENERAL:

What a farce! It's so sad.

DOCTOR:

Yes, General. Darkness is falling. We must sound the curfew.
Singing a little flat.
Da da! Da da! Da di di da di di da. . . .

GENERAL:

Stop that! What do you take me for? That's the Infantry Lights Out!

DOCTOR:

Making conversation.
I beg your pardon. Eh—how does it go exactly—in the cavalry?

GENERAL:

In a cracked voice.
Da di! Da di! Da. . . . I haven't the heart for it. It's too silly.
Softly.
Lieutenant St. Pé. I want to live. I want to love. I want to give my heart as well, dear God!

123]

DOCTOR:

General, nobody wants it any more. Let it unswell quietly, that old over-tender sponge. You should have sown fewer wild oats and had the courage to hurt while there was still time. Life should be led like a cavalry charge, General. They ought to have told you that at Saumur. My poor old friend, shall I tell you the moral of this story? One must never understand one's enemy or one's wife. One must never understand anyone for that matter, or one will die of it. Heigh-ho, I must go home to Mme. Bonfant and her scenes. I think you will do very nicely on your own.

He pats him on the shoulder.

See you very soon.

GENERAL:

Motionless.

Yes, yes.

The DOCTOR goes.

GENERAL'S WIFE:

Off.

Leon!

GENERAL:

Yes.

VOICE:

Are you there?

GENERAL:

Yes.

[124

VOICE:

Good. I'm going to have a little nap. Don't do anything in the meantime.

GENERAL:

No.

He shudders and cries suddenly.

Lieutenant St. Pé. Graduated second from Saumur! Take aim! Steady! Fire!

He stands quite still. A shadow appears on the terrace, holding a broom. It is the new MAID.

MAID:

Did you call, sir?

GENERAL:

Starting.

Eh? What? No, I didn't call. Who are you?

MAID:

I'm the new girl, sir. The new chambermaid you engaged this morning.

GENERAL:

Looking at her absently, then stroking his moustache.

Ah yes, of course, by Jove, yes, yes. What was I thinking of? And what is your name, my dear?

MAID:

Pamela, sir.

GENERAL:

Pamela. Fancy that now. Pamela. And the prettiest bosom in the world too. What is all this nonsense

125]

about our having a soul? Do you believe in it? He's a fool, that doctor. Put your broom down, my child. It's a bit late to be sweeping up now. And there is never enough dust on things. We must let it settle. You know, you'll find this an easy sort of place. I'm an old youngster and I don't ask for very much—provided folks are nice to me. You haven't seen my roses, have you? Come, I'll show you round the garden, and if you're a good girl I'll give you one. It doesn't bother you, does it, Pamela, if I put my arm round your waist?

MAID:

Coyly.
No, sir, but what will Madam say?

GENERAL:

Madam will say nothing so long as you don't tell her. That's a good girl. It's nicer like this, don't you think? Not that it means anything, but still, one feels less lonely, in the dark.

They go out, an absurd couple, into the dark garden. "Lights Out"—the cavalry's this time —is heard in the distance, played by a distant bugle in some barracks in the town, and:

The curtain falls.